2 Superbag

This bag is a good way to disguise any gift, whatever its shape.
  It looks particularly clever if you make each bag in two sorts of paper.
That's also a good way to combine leftover pieces of wrapping paper or mix
plain brown with something more extravagantly Christmassy.

1 Cut a rectangle of paper large enough to hide the gift with plenty to spare. Fold in half lengthways and crease.

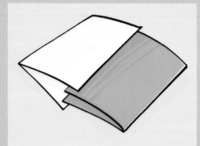

2 Cut another rectangle, 1cm larger than the first, and fold in half lengthways. Overlap the smaller piece on the larger piece by the 1cm extra. Be sure you line up the pieces perfectly straight and tape together.

3 Cut a sliver like this from the bottom edge. Turn up the corners and fold up the bottom edge with a 1.5cm turn. Then tape.

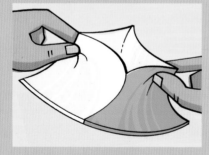

4 Insert your gift. Then squeeze the top edges so the side creases meet in the middle. Tape the top closed like this either with transparent tape over the top or a narrow piece of double-sided tape on the inside.

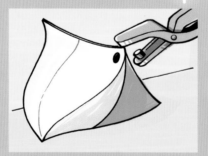

5 Punch a hole in one corner (avoiding the gift) and tie in decorations. Choose leftover yarn, string, wool, beads, and buttons as you fancy. Be careful not to tear the hole.

You can make a simpler bag with a single piece of paper if you prefer, and fold the top edge as you did the bottom edge.

3 Starry gift tag

These gift tags make even a plainly wrapped gift look festive. Each one only uses a small piece of card and thread.

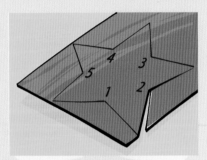

1 Cut a five-point star using the template on the back cover. Imagine each valley between the points having a number, as shown above (or write the numbers on a practice star).

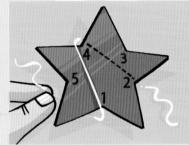

2 Cut a piece of yarn 60cm long. Now hold it at valley one, with a shorter end left for the tie and the longer end for winding.

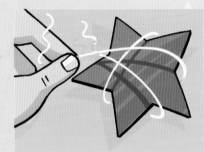

3 Wind from valley to valley as shown in the chart. When you get back to 1, tie a knot close to the valley.

4 If you wish, decorate your star by gluing on cut or punched bits of card. Write your message on the back before tying the tag to a parcel.

Winding chart:
over from 1 to 4
under from 4 to 2
over from 2 to 5
under from 5 to 3
over from 3 to 1
under from 1 to 4
over from 4 to 2
under from 2 to 5
over from 5 to 3
under back to 1

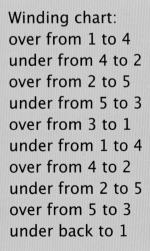

You could also use this style of star as a tree decoration.

Why not cut your tags from card you might throw away, such as pretty packaging and colourful bits of Christmas cards?

4 Beautiful boxes

All kinds of things come packaged in good cardboard boxes. They can be reused as containers for gifts, and it's easy to add a few touches to make them beautiful.

1 Take a box and paint it all over with gesso. Once it is dry (which won't take long), add another coat. You may need to apply several coats to get a good finish.

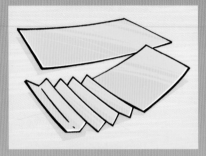

2 Select a piece of bright paper (it doesn't matter if it has printing on one side) and cut a piece about three times as long as it is wide: try 6cm x 18cm. Zigzag fold as evenly as you can to gather up the length.

3 Take a piece of coloured yarn long enough to tie easily round the box. Find the centre and place the zigzag piece here. Knot the yarn to hold the folds so they don't get crushed.

4 The paper will fan out like a bow tie. Hold the ends so the tips meet. Fasten these with a piece of sticky tape on the underside or use double-sided tape.

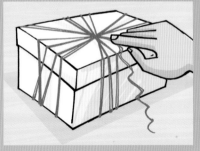

5 Put the gift in the box and the lid on top. Now wrap lengths of coloured yarn as shown and tie. Finally, tie in your decoration.

You can *save your boxes and reuse* them time and again, repainting if needed.

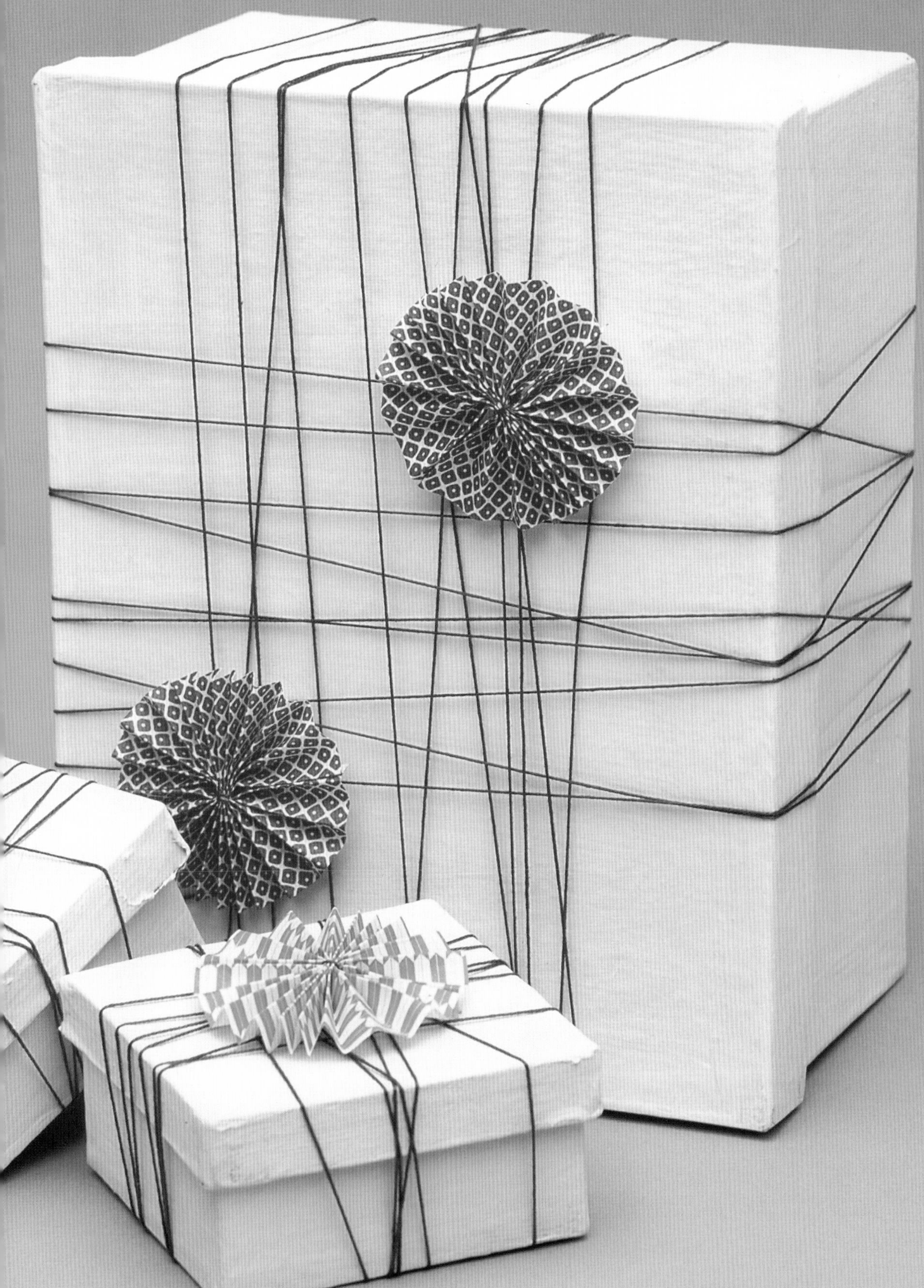

5 Festive bunting

Deck the halls and all along the walls with bright flags in Christmas colours.

This craft makes the most of one side of white A4 paper, much used in offices. If you hang bunting against a wall, it doesn't matter to have writing on the "wrong" side, and it should be easy to get hold of plenty of paper.

1 Rule a line about 2cm along one long side of A4 paper. Then fold in half along the long side and crease. Unfold.

2 Mark the centre point along the lower edge of the two panels. Use a pale pencil crayon to rule lines from the top corner to the centre point to mark the shape of bunting flags.

3 Decorate the flags in Christmas colours. You want lots of flags, so go for designs that are quick to paint: stripes, checks, and big dots. Leave to dry.

Enjoy painting these flags quickly. That way the designs will look bright and lively.

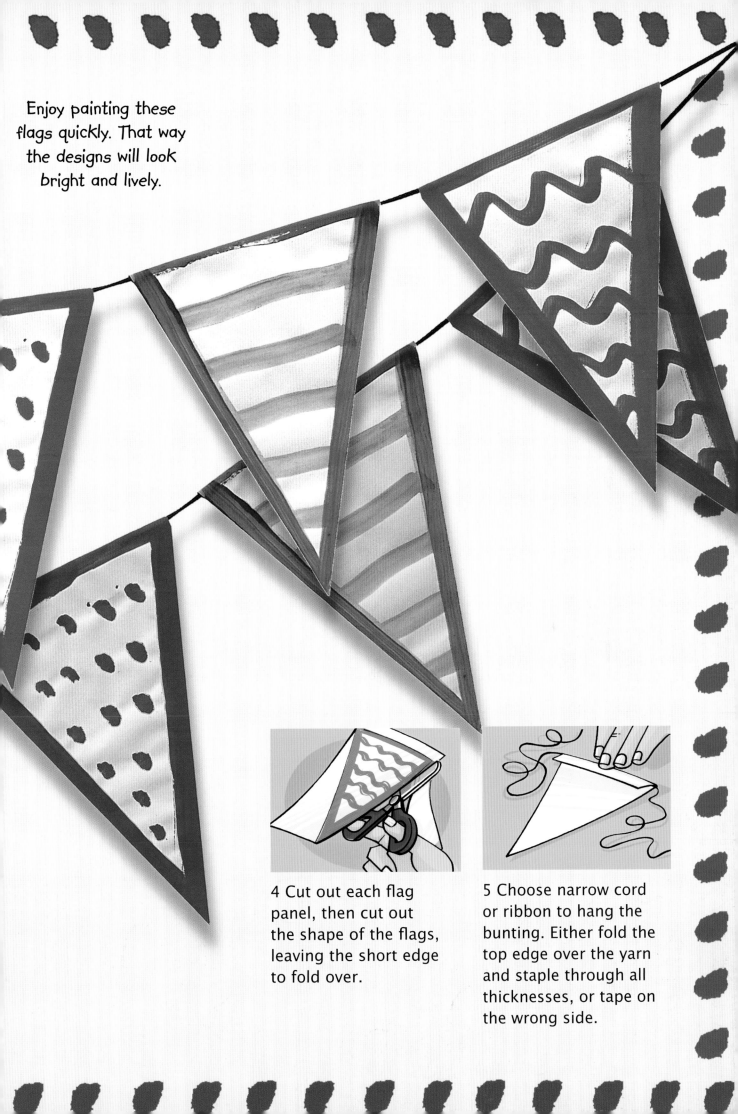

4 Cut out each flag panel, then cut out the shape of the flags, leaving the short edge to fold over.

5 Choose narrow cord or ribbon to hang the bunting. Either fold the top edge over the yarn and staple through all thicknesses, or tape on the wrong side.

6 Beautiful baubles

These balls are simple to make from tiny amounts of paper. You could hang them up, simply adding a loop at the top. Or you could pile them in a bowl for a table centrepiece.

 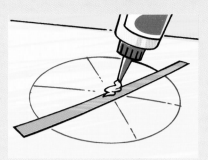 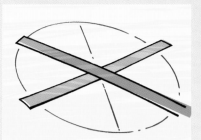

1 Cut strips of tough paper or thin card. A good size is 1.5cm x 20cm. You will need three for each bauble. Mark the centre point of each.

2 Take the first piece and add a dab of glue or a snip of double-sided tape at the centre point on the wrong side. Lay it wrong side up on the layout guide on the back cover, matching the centres.

3 Take the second piece and add glue or tape at the centre point on the wrong side. Lay it on top the first piece wrong side up but at the next line on the layout guide, matching the centres.

Add a hanging loop through the top if you wish to put these baubles on the tree.

 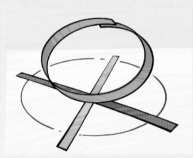

4 Lay the third piece on top at the final point on the layout guide.

5 Now take both ends of the first piece, curl them up, and glue or tape them together. Repeat for the other two pieces.

7 Tree for ever

A tree with a root won't actually last for ever, but it will last many Christmases.

It's best to begin with quite a small tree that will be happy in a pot for several years.

1 Choose an evergreen tree with a Christmassy shape. Plant it in a square pot, beginning with a few pebbles at the bottom and adding potting compost, or compost and soil.

2 Put a cane or stick in each corner so as to make a pyramid that is taller than the tree. Tie this with string.

3 Thread bells or decorations on string and tie them from the top.

4 Add bows of bright ribbon at the top and at each corner. Remember you can keep these from year to year.

Hanging stars

Weave these simple stars in card to hang on a tree.
  You could choose a colour scheme as shown here, or mix plain card with strips from brightly coloured packaging.

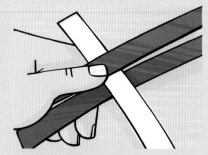

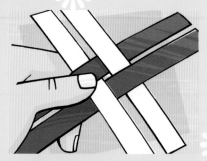

1 Cut strips of stiff card, each 30cm x 1.5cm. You will need two for each star. Choose a pair and cut them in half – to give a pair of each colour.

2 Take two strips and hold them like this. Now take a third strip and weave it over and under the two you are holding.

3 Weave the fourth strip under and over. Adjust the position of the strips to make a neat square in the middle of the star.

If the star is wobbly before it is woven, add a tiny piece of masking tape to the centre to hold it. Remove the tape once the weaving is done.

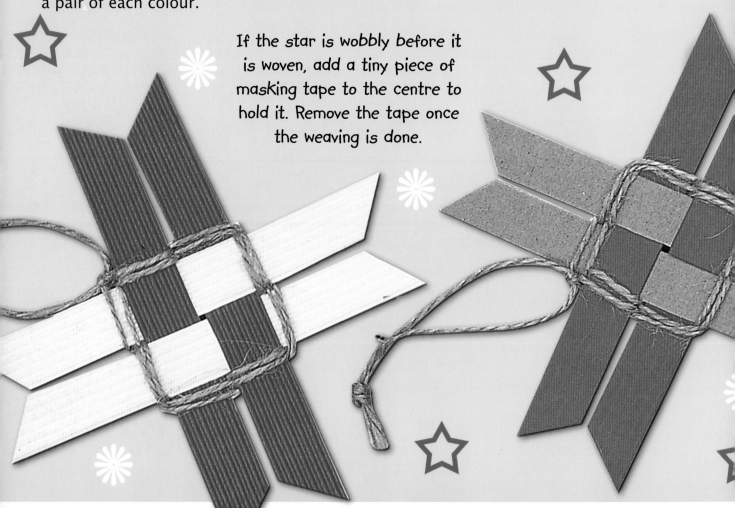

4 Now take a piece of yarn 60cm long. Leaving a short end as a tie and starting at one corner, begin weaving clockwise around the pieces so that the overs and unders counter balance the overs and unders in the card weaving.

5 When you reach the starting corner, twist the yarn over the shorter yarn and go back anticlockwise so the overs and unders counterbalance the overs and unders in the first round.

6 When you reach the corner, twist the yarn over the shorter yarn and go clockwise again. When you reach the corner, twist and go anticlockwise. Then tie the two ends together. Trim and snip the card ends.

9 Wreathed in green

This traditional decoration uses only clippings from living plants. Even evergreen leaves will fade once they are cut, so this is best made for your main festive day.

Of course, the cut leaves can be composted!

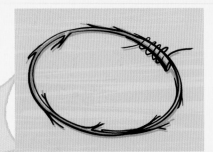

1 Find or make a circular frame. One of the simplest ways is to ask a grown-up to help you bend a wire coat hanger into a circle, or you can tie lengths of bendy twig with raffia.

2 Cut small lengths of evergreen and tie them into bundles. Choose Christmas plants such as pine, fir, holly, and ivy. You will need enough to go round the frame with the leaves of each bundle overlapping the stems of the bundle in front.

3 Tie each bundle onto the circular frame in two places: once near the cut ends, and once at least 5cm further up the stem. Add a ribbon bow to each bundle (if you wish) before you tie in the bundle behind.

You can hang all kinds of decorations from a ceiling wreath.

10 Festive shortbread

This traditional festive treat makes a great gift.

Choose packaging that has the least possible impact on the environment. Cellophane looks glamorous but, being made from wood, biodegrades more quickly than plastic.

Ask a grown-up before you attempt any cooking, and wash your hands.

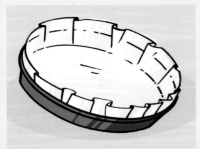

1 Select a cake tin about 20cm in diameter and line it with a circle of greaseproof paper, leaving a frill around the edge. Heat the oven to 160°C.

2 Measure into a bowl 120g plain flour, 30g ground almonds and 100g sugar. Then add in 100g butter cut into cubes.

3 Mix the butter into the dry ingredients with your fingers, breaking the butter into tinier and tinier pieces and then squeezing the mix. After about 5 minutes it will form a lump.

4 Place the lump in the tin and press out to fill the circle. Prick it all over with a fork. Bake the cookie for about 15 minutes or until lightly browned.

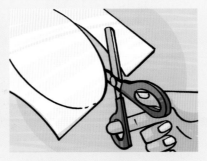

5 Leave the cookie to cool. Meanwhile, cut two circles a little larger than the cookie from strong card (perhaps cut from packaging) so together they make a strong base. Tape them together in three places around the edge.

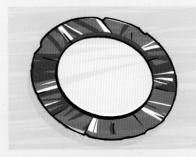

6 Cut a larger circle of cellophane and tape it over surface of the card, using sticky tape to hold it down on the underside.

7 Then take a large rectangle of cellophane and tape that in place on the underside too. Turn the base right side up.

8 Slide the cookie onto the base and trim away the greaseproof paper. Wrap the rectangle of cellophane over and over. Then tie the ends with yarn, ribbon, or raffia and frill them out.

11 Sweet treats

These marzipan sweets can be filled with your favourite goodies.
Ask a grown-up before you attempt any cooking, and wash your hands.

1 Line a baking tray with greaseproof paper. Heat the oven to 160°C. Then grate the rind of a lemon on to a plate.

2 Mix in a bowl 200g ground almonds, 100g icing sugar,100g golden caster sugar, and the lemon rind. Mix the ingredients together with one egg to form a ball.

3 Divide the ball into about 12 smaller balls. Then shape each of these into a "cup".

4 Place your choice of treat in each cup: try chopped nuts, chopped glacé cherries, raisins, or chopped chocolate. Gather the edges and roll to enclose the filling.

5 Place the balls on the baking tray and top with a cherry or nuts. Place the tray in the oven and bake for 10–12 minutes. Allow to cool before tasting, as the filling may be hot.

You can present your treats on a plate or, to give as a gift, place in a reused glass jar.

12 Leaf notebooks

These leaf-shaped notebooks are useful little gifts. They are a clever way to reuse good bits of paper cut from letters, envelopes and packaging. The leaf print is a reminder to be careful about using paper so as not to squander trees.

Get in the habit of collecting bits and pieces of plain paper and card from leftovers. To do this craft, you should also collect scrap paper to protect your printing area.

1 Collect good leaves in summer or autumn and, if you are not ready to print, press them between unwanted scraps of paper with a heavy book on top. Choose several of each kind that are similar.

2 When you are ready, protect your printing area with layers of scrap paper. Put paint on a plate. Lightly brush on the underside of a leaf. Lay it paint side up.

3 Now press a piece of good scrap on the painted leaf: press, lift, and peel. You may get two or three prints from one application of paint, and you can reuse a leaf several times. Print enough of each species of leaf for a single notebook, plus cover pieces on card.

Cut extra "leaves" on plain paper to make a notebook fatter easily.

4 When the paint is dry, trace a simple shape around the leaf type you have chosen. Note where the stalk and leaf tip go. Glue the tracing on to card and cut it out, making a snipped V each end to mark the stalk and tip.

5 Draw round the card on all the leaf prints of the same type, using the snipped V to help you position the template. Cut out the leaves.

6 Gather your leaves into notebooks, with the plain side up for jotting on. Add the card covers top and bottom. Thread string, twine, or wire through the hole.

13 Reduce your stocking footprint

Christmas can get a bit over-extravagant. Have fun giving and receiving just a few fun gifts by choosing to make smaller stockings.

1 Draw a stocking shape on paper and note the lines for toe and cuff. Cut a paper pattern piece for these shapes.

2 Pin the pattern shapes on to a double layer of felt, choosing contrasting colours. Cut them out. Also cut out a decorative shape, such as a heart.

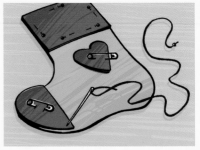

3 Take one stocking shape and use safety pins to hold the decorative pieces in place. Thread a thickish needle with bright yarn and make a knot at the end.

4 Stitch the pieces in place with a stab stitch, stabbing the needle straight down through the layers then straight up before pulling the tail. Do the same with the other stocking shape.

5 Now stitch the two stocking shapes together. Ask a grown-up to help you fasten the top corners with overlapping stitches. Add a hanging loop if you wish.

14 Thank-you note

Here is a simple way to make a Christmas thank-you note. It's inexpensive to make, but the thank you is worth more than anything.

1 On plain paper you can write on, draw a square 10cm x 10cm and cut it out.

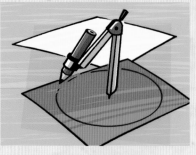

2 Select outer paper in two colours. Ask a grown-up to help you use compasses to draw four circles, each with a 5cm radius (half the side of the square.)

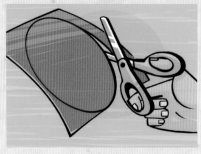

3 Cut out the four circles. Fold each in half, crease, and uncrease.

4 Hold one folded semicircle in place along a side of the square piece. Add a semicircle in the other colour along the next side so that it underlaps the first piece on the underside and overlaps on the upper side.

5 Add the remaining semicircles in the same way. Check that they are interwoven on both sides and then fasten the underside with a peelable sticker or cut-out shape that you glue on.

6 Unfold the top side, write your note, then interlap the semicircles back in place.

7 Add a sticker to fasten the centre or glue on a shape. Or you can tie your note with string, yarn, or ribbon.

15 Boxing Day box

Reduce, reuse, recycle: these are the watchwords of living in a way that is kind to the planet.

Make a big and beautiful box from reused materials: in it you can keep all the leftover bits and pieces from one Christmas to use again – perhaps many times!

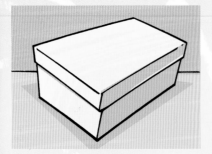

1 Select a large and sturdy cardboard box with a lid. If this is hard to find, look out for two boxes, one slightly larger than the other. Ask a grown-up to help cut them so one is a lid for the other.

2 Glue brown paper over the edges of the box and lid to bind them. Do the same to patch any holes or gaps.

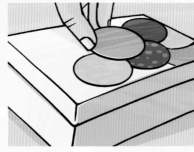

3 Cut circles about 10cm in diameter from scraps of Christmas paper, or even bright pictures from magazines. A quick way is to draw around a bowl. Cut these out.

4 Brush glue on the underside of each circle and glue onto the box and its lid. Overlap the circles so you cover the entire box.

Pack your box carefully at the end of Christmas so it is a real delight to reopen the next Christmas. Include ribbons, good bits of paper, and pretty clippings.

Tie your box shut with string or ribbon.

5 Cut or punch stars from contrasting paper, or cut smaller circles in this colour. Glue these on.

16 Ecostar

These simple stars are folded from twigs. You need to choose twigs that are supple and, when folded into points, snap only part-way through. Birch and willow are suitable and readily available.

Weaving the twigs under on the last length will help hold the star in place.

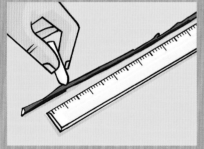

1 Cut a thin, straight twig about 42cm long. Imagine fold points at 12cm, 6cm, 6cm, 6cm, and 12cm (you can mark these with chalk if you like).

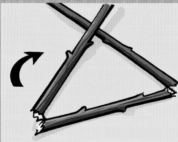

2 Fold into a five-pointed star, weaving over and under as the twig allows.

3 Fasten th ends with t tie with ya Trim the l you wish.